StarLost

Ariel Giacobbe

BookLeaf Publishing

India | USA | UK

Presentation by *BookLeaf Publishing*

Web: www.bookleafpub.com

E-mail: info@bookleafpub.com

ISBN: 9789358311365

First edition 2023

HARKER, 0800

I step onto the shimmering silver surface of the
space station
Thousands of stars reflect back at me across the
curves of the dome
I feel the grin on my face as I look around at the
other explorers
The sensation of being connected by a love of
the unknown is warm, dazzling
My skin is made of crystals reaching for the
light of the suns in the distance
Excited and dancing as the universe blankets me
in its embrace
A lifetime of gazing up at the night sky
whispers, I'm exactly where I'm meant to be

VALON, 0800

There's a strange weightlessness as I emerge
from the ship onto the station
I can feel it in my stomach, in my lungs, in my
fingertips
The air has a taste, one of the elements mixing
with the pull of an empty vacuum of time
The quiet beyond calls to me, replaced by a
sudden, swarming cascade of voices
I'm lost in a pool of bodies, all wanting and
eager
My breathing constricts, and I squeeze toward
an unoccupied length of corridor
The stretch of cold metal calms me, allowing the
buzzing in my mind to fade to a dull ache

HARKER, 0805

The other explorers are a beautiful constellation
of hope, woven together by invisible, iridescent
heartstrings
I wade through, collecting handshakes like
crystalized comets pulled from positive energy
As I reach the starport on the far side, my eyes
drift to a corridor pocketed by shadows
She stands at the end of it, made of curves and
waves of midnight hair cascading down her back
Everything about her is voluminous, from her
curls to her hips to her dewy lips
Her eyes catch mine, dark pools deep and
endless, tugging me into her field of gravity
We meet in the middle, two planets circling in
orbit, humming and pulsing, the tingling
nearness of heavenly bodies

VALON, 0805

The noise of the others frays at my nerves,
threatening to spill over
I breathe in, willing calm to wash over me,
squeezing eyes shut
When I breathe out, my vision comes back into
focus and I see her
Framed by the starport, she blots out the rest of
the world
Behind her an indigo, cerise, and lilac nebula
swirls, the same colors of her cloud-shaped tufts
of hair
The warmth in her eyes matches their deep
lavender shade as her soft pink lips ease into a
smile
Somehow I've drifted closer to her, and in my
mind we're floating in a sea of sparkling stars,
immune to gravity and time

HARKER, 0806

She's as alluring as the sun, brightening my
world from inches away
Light radiates from within her, cresting over me,
sending tingles along my skin
My fingers close around hers as our hands touch
in greeting
There's no shake, only a gentle touch of
introduction, palm meeting palm
All at once, I'm alive and streaking through the
atmosphere, nerves awoken that have only
known sleep until now
Instead of parting, we feel the weight of each
other, lingering and hovering in arcs of pressing
closer and bending just out of reach
Inside, I'm a supernova, exploding with
sensations ready to be explored

VALON, 0806

Something in me reaches out for her, a desire to
be known
It's new and so unlike me, I'm a foreign object in
wild space, yet to be discovered
Asteroids crash and break apart in my stomach,
a nervous energy surprisingly welcome
The ominous, anxious weight on my chest is
missing, replaced by the lightness of stardust
My thumb acts on its own accord, tracing a path
across her knuckles, down the smooth skin of
her narrow wrist
I want to remember this, log it in my mind,
freeze the memory into an immortalized echo
She squeezes my hand and I squeeze back,
opening up to the possibility of an us

HARKER, 0807

A distant voice breaks in through the glittering
haze, calling out for attention
They're briefing us, assigning us our regions
The places we'll be exploring, those unknowable
areas of space
Planets alive and breathing outside of the worlds
we've touched
This dream I've had for a lifetime is suddenly
within my grasp
No distance has ever scared me or made me
question my path
Yet standing before her, I wonder if lightyears
seem further when she's outside of reach

VALON, 0807

All I've ever wanted is up on that screen with its
glowing, blinding light
The one with the names of every explorer,
followed by the name of their region of
everchanging space
It will tell me where I'll be, where I'll make my
temporary new home
I never cared where I was sent, I never cared
what I would see
The joy was in the newness, whatever it held,
whatever shape it took, whatever it could be
Yet I ache for a moment, thinking it'd tear me
from her
Then, I see my region, Arrayus, and find it
mirrored in her eyes as they meet mine: we're
written in the stars

HARKER, 2322

That night, in the barracks, my mind is an
electric storm, crackling with thoughts of her
She lays in the bunk across from mine,
illuminated only by the starshine in the viewport
Her dark hair is a beautiful cloud around her
head, her face, her shoulders
It wisps around her arms and down her back,
hiding and highlighting her at the same time
Her curves aren't lessened by the blanket atop
her, they're heightened
The thin fabric showcases the dips and valleys
of her waist, her chest, her hips
She's made of slopes and canyons, strong, firm,
and soft all at once

VALON, 2323

I'm used to my thoughts strangling me at night,
reaching cold hands up and into my mind
This is different, the ones of her are warm, like
the welcome presence of the moon hanging in
the sky
Breathing deep, I risk a glance in her direction,
desperate to know if she's asleep in her bed
Bright indigo eyes shine in the dark, their
otherworldly glow filling me with their magic
I can feel her smile more than see it, it's open
and inviting me in
The tug is low in my belly, a string tying me to
her well of gravity
I'm not afraid of rejection as I reach out my hand
toward her in the night, letting it hover in the
empty space between our bunks

HARKER, 2334

There's no hesitation in her movements, no
doubt or second guessing
My response is immediate, eager and longing to
close the unnatural empty air between us
It's palpable, this field tugging us in, sparking
around our fingertips as our pinkies touch
Winding together as the rest of our fingers
interlace, weaving into patterns of caramel and
honey
Her midnight gaze is an eclipse, blocking out
everything that isn't her
It cannot be confused for a hidden, forbidden
moment, it's real, open, and blossoming in
moonlight
I am safe, accepted, wild with possibility

VALON, 2335

A calm I have not known before overtakes me as
she accepts my invitation
This seemingly small gesture of hand in hand
feels like the grandest in the universe
I'm painted in greens of earth, blues of oceans,
and rosy skies of worlds left behind
We're sailing into the eternal stretch of space
bathed in the peaceful hum of home
I'm meant to be here, with her hand in mine,
breathing the same stretch of air
The joy is all over my face, open and
unapologetic as I let sleep overtake me
Instead of keeping it locked away, I let the
happiness flood in, allowing myself to feel each
inch of it's big, bountiful surface

HARKER, 1003

The journey to Arrayus is filled with echoing
chimes of anticipation
A chorus of chords zing and strum in my ears as
I watch a thousand stars skip by
We slip into the system, met with a mesmerizing
orb of smokey pastels
The first planet for us to explore is a stunning
expanse of pale blues and unlocked lilacs
Valon is beside me in her spacesuit, beginning
the descent to the mystery of the surface
Drifting down together through uncharted space
overwhelms me with a weightless joy
She circles me in a gravityless dance, suits
protecting and connecting so much more than
our bodies

VALON, 1009

The blinding horizon fills my helmet as we pass
into the clouded atmosphere
This is it, my first glimpse of a new world, made
a million star systems better by the unveiled
exuberance of Harker
Soft pink light of a cotton candy sky comes into
view, illuminated further by the cool blue of dual
moons and a pale yellow sun
Lavender grasses are dotted by violet flowers
that frame the edges of clear, teal waters rippling
into winding rivers and shallow pools
Ivory trees cast shade over chalk colored cliffs,
casting gray shadows and washing the hills in
shades of purple
As I watch Harker float into the planet's
embrace, I see her colors reflected back at her
She's a physical embodiment of this wondrous,
alien world, opening up for me to explore

HARKER, 1016

My foot makes contact with the ground, sinking
into its squishy, mossy surface
It's steady yet yielding, leaving me both
balanced and light on my toes
The readings in my helmet allow me to remove
it without doubt, to breathe in deep
A sugary, sweet scent envelopes me instantly,
lingering on my tongue like whipped meringue
I can taste the spun taffy colors, real and robust
as the silky petals of flowers drifting through the
air
Slipping out of the lingering remains of my suit,
I stretch my fingertips out to touch the satin
smooth surfaces of grasses and crisp, crystal
waters
Everything is a hazy memory, new and foreign,
yet invoking of something I've always known

VALON, 1025

Watching Harker slide off her spacesuit fills me
with breathless terror
My heart tightens, ready to blast apart, a laser
tearing through an asteroid
Panic and fear often live in my mind, but never
has their grip wound around my chest
The roaring in my ears lessens as I realize she's
safe, alive and shining
Euphoria radiates from her body, replacing any
doubt in me with elation
I allow myself to embrace this place of
discovery, the one I've strived toward for a
lifetime
A world I can learn, study, and grow from,
expansive enough to spend cycles on with
Harker if we choose

HARKER, 1027

I'm spinning, my arms open, bathing in the soft,
golden light blanketing the woods and fields
My upturned face drinks in the glowing caress
of the double moons, day and night mingled into
one
Stars are sprinkled through the swirling,
changing sky, mixed amongst fluffy cherry
blossom clouds
The wide open space spans out, each direction
more intoxicating than the last
Most vivid of all are Valon's galaxy eyes on
mine, host to the whole universe of her
We step together, developing our own rhythm,
our own pattern of interstellar movements
Our destiny is woven in colliding stars,
consuming us in a wash of time-bending fate

VALON, 1028

There's no space between us as I touch my
fingers to hers, guiding hands to thumbs, to
wrists, to arms
My nerves are alive, pulsing, tingling, directing
me how to trace a path from her wide shoulders
to her sculpted collarbone to her arched neck
These feelings I thought I'd never know are
pouring over me, dousing me in their glow
I'm an explorer on an unknown world, learning
the pathways and unpaved roads with awe and
delighted surprise
We lean in, breath mingling, closing the gaps,
molding, mirroring, twin suns locked in rotation
Her lips are a brush, painting mine with shooting
stars and comets, burning their way across the
galaxy
Their satin touch is curves and pillows, tasting
of the same cotton candy as the air, melting on
my tongue

HARKER, 1041

I scoop her river of curls into my palm,
clutching their glossy, springy surface
Their darkness is composed of every color: reds,
browns, and blacks, woven with deep amethysts
and azures
My other hand fits on the shelf of her waist, the
wide arch of her sensuous hips
The kiss deepens, allowing me to soar through
the solar system at the speed of light
Stars are shining and expanding beneath my
eyelids with each move, each sound
I lean back to look at her, drink her in like liquid
sunlight
She's clearer and more visible than anything I've
seen, an unwavering beam through a nebulous
mist

VALON, 1045

Instead of shrinking under her gaze, I let it wash
over me, guiding and matching it
I bathe in the moment, committing every inch of
her to memory, not out of fear, but anticipation
of what's to come
This is something I want to add to the infinite
story of me, of her, of us
Above, the stars are frozen at certain moments in
time, where we join them, cementing our place
in the constellations
I lean my forehead to hers, grounding myself
and listening to the gentle beat of her heart as
mine matches its time
She's the beacon calling me home, guiding me
after years adrift in space
For the first time, I'm rooted, ready to stay and
embrace what's before me

HARKER, 1050

I kiss her again, lightly, gently, a promise of so
much more on the horizon
Our hands intertwine, connecting us as we begin
our great journey across the planet's surface
The promise of discovery is in and around us,
expanding out into all of Arrayus
We create the map as we go, charting each
flower, each crater, each experience
The spirit of exploration is in every delighted
smile, excited touch, shared sensation
I am not lost in her, nor is she lost in me
Together, we are found, in this place, in this
time, and we're exactly where we're meant to be